BRAINTE AND
FOR GRITTY KIDS

3OO Difficult Mind-Bending Lateral Thinking, Logic, and Math Puzzles for Kids and Families

created by Dan Allbaugh

1

Copyright © 2024
ISBN: 979-8-9898301-2-1

Green Meeple Books

greenmeeplebooks.com

GRITTY KIDS

for ages 4-6

for ages 6-10

for ages 8-12

for ages 8-10

for ages 10-12

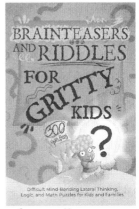

for all ages

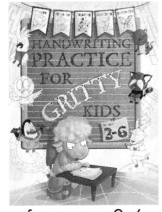

for ages 3-6

for ages 5+

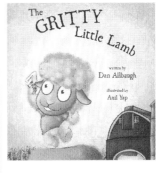

for ages 3-8

Table of Contents

INTRODUCTION

Working through brainteasers not only boosts problem-solving skills but also enhances memory, learning abilities, and strengthens grit by demanding sustained effort and focus. This collection of fun riddles is designed to stretch thinking by forcing minds to exercise differently from conventional learning. Inside you'll find:

Lateral Thinking Riddles: Challenges that require an indirect or creative approach to view problems from unique angles.
Logic Riddles: Questions that hone cognitive skills through rationalization and deduction.
Math Riddles: Puzzles that involve mindful thought, reasoning, and calculation.

These riddle types are mixed throughout and sometimes resemble each other, so approach each question with careful consideration! The book is organized into three chapters that progressively become more challenging, with answers provided in the back when the brain needs a little nudge.

Perfect for children and engaging for all ages, this book is a delightful mental workout that the whole family will enjoy.

*"I cannot teach anybody anything.
I can only make them think."*

-Socrates

TRICKY RIDDLES

1. First, think of the color of the clouds. Next, think of the color of snow. Now, think of the color of a bright full moon. Now answer quickly: what do cows drink?

2. Which is the most curious letter?

3. What has a face and two hands but no arms or legs?

4. Take off my skin - I won't cry, but you will! What am I?

5. I love to dance and twist and prance, I shake my tail, as away I sail, wingless I fly into the sky. What am I?

6. What is the softest nut?

7. What's always freezing, but never wears a coat?

8. What kind of button can't be unbuttoned?

9. I get smaller every time I take a bath. What am I?

10. What has a neck but no head?

11. The more of this there is, the less you see. What is it?

12. What building has more stories than any others in the neighborhood?

13. Rich people need it, Poor people have it, And if you eat it you will die. What is it?

14. What runs out when you push it too far?

15. There's a one-story house where everything is yellow. The walls are yellow. The doors are yellow. Even the furniture is yellow. What color are the stairs?

16. I'm so simple, I only point. Yet I guide people all over the world. What am I?

17. What has ears but cannot hear?

18. I have branches, but no fruit, trunk, or leaves. What am I?

19. Three different doctors said that Paul is their brother yet Paul claims he has no brothers. Who is lying?

20. What can you catch, but not throw?

21. What has a head, a tail, but no body?

22. What kind of band never plays music?

23. When writing the sequence of numbers 1 through 100, how many times will you write the number 7?

24. I fly without wings, I cry without eyes. Whenever I go, darkness flies. What am I?

25. I make a loud sound when I'm changing. When I do change, I get bigger but weigh less. What am I?

26. A man is pushing his car along a road when he comes to a hotel. He shouts, "I'm bankrupt!" Why?

27. What has one eye, but can't see?

28. Which word is written incorrectly in the dictionary?

29. What goes up and down but doesn't move?

30. What can be cracked, made, told, and played?

31. If you put your finger in my eye, my jaws will open wide. What am I?

32. How many numbers between 1-100 have the letter 'a' in their spelling?

33. What kind of room has no doors or windows?

34. Which word, if pronounced right, is wrong, but if pronounced wrong is right?

35. What gets wetter as it dries?

36. What can go up but never comes down?

37. What has four wheels and flies?

38. What invention lets you look right through a wall?

39. What is easy to get into, but hard to get out of?

40. What can be touched but can't be seen?

41. You can throw me off the highest building in the world and I will not break. But my life ends if you place me gently in the ocean. What am I?

42. I'm where yesterday follows today and tomorrow is in the middle. What am I?

43. What tastes better than it smells?

44. What's found on the ground but never gets dirty?

45. I pass before the sun, yet make no shadow. What am I?

46. What can be filled with empty hands?

47. I go around in circles, but always straight ahead never complain, no matter where I am led. What am I?

48. What ring is square?

49. I do not have eyes but I once could see. I used to have thoughts but now I'm empty. What am I?

50. If you put roast in a roaster, what do you put in toaster?

51. What has many keys but cannot open a single lock?

52. What has many teeth but cannot bite?

53. Some months have 30 days, and some months have 31 days. How many have 28?

54. If I have three apples and you take away two, how many do you have?

55. What can you see every night without asking, but by morning is gone without being taken?

56. If you don't keep it, it will break. What is it?

57. What gets larger the more you take away from it?

58. What three positive numbers give the same result whether they are all multiplied or added together?

59. What has four legs but never walks?

tricky riddles questions

60. Before Mount Everest was discovered, what was the highest mountain the world?

61. What has a neck with no head and two arms but no hands?

62. How far can a squirrel run into the woods?

63. What is harder to catch the faster you run?

64. What is always in front of you but can't be seen?

65. What does not eat food but still enjoys a light meal every day?

66. Which tire doesn't move when a car turns right?

67. What gets sharper the more you use it?

68. What belongs to you but others use it more than you do?

69. What is it that you can keep after giving it to someone else?

70. What kind of coat is always wet when you put it on?

71. What can you hold in your left hand but not in your right hand?

72. What has a ring but no finger?

73. People buy me to eat, but never eat me. What am I?

74. Tear one off and scratch my head, what once was red is black instead! What am I?

75. What is it something that you always have but you always leave behind?

76. What doesn't get any wetter, no matter how much rain falls on it?

77. What loses its head in the morning but gets it back at night?

78. I am as simple as a circle, worthless as a leader; but when I follow a group, their strength increases tenfold. By myself I'm practically nothing. What am I?

79. What flies around all day but never goes anywhere?

80. What never asks any question but still gets answered?

81. When can a net hold water?

82. A runner competing in a race overtakes the runner in fifth position. What position are they in now?

83. One candy cane has two ends. How many ends do two and a half candy canes have?

tricky riddles questions

84. Grace had the 50th best and 50th worst test scores in her class. How many students were in her class?

85. A man fell from a 30-foot ladder but didn't get hurt. How is that possible?

86. What year do Christmas and New Year's Day fall in the same year?

87. What kinds of stones are never found in the ocean?

88. What can travel around the world but never leaves its corner?

89. A man was walking in the rain. He was in the middle of nowhere. He had nothing and nowhere to hide. He came home all wet, but not a single hair on his head was wet. Why is that?

90. What is seen in the middle of March and April that can't be seen at the beginning or end of either month?

91. What begins with T, ends with T, and has T in it?

92. What goes through cities and fields but never moves?

93. A dog is tied to a 10-meter rope but is able to reach a bone that is 15 meters away. How?

94. What question can you ask all day long and always get completely different answers that are always correct?

95. You draw a line. Without touching it, how do you make the line longer?

96. As you sit down for breakfast and realize you have four bagels left. If you eat one per day, you'll run out in four days so you cut them in half. How many bagels do you have now?

97. What is served but never eaten?

98. What is something that you can give away but you still get to keep?

99. If you have a 10-meter string and it takes 2 seconds to cut a 1-meter piece, how long will it take to cut the entire string?

100. He has one and a person has two, a citizen has three and a human being has four, a personality has five and an inhabitant of earth has six. What am I?

101. Tread on the living, they make not a mumble. Tread on the dead, they mutter and grumble. What are they?

102. What is made of water but if you put it into water it will die?

103. What three-letter seed still sounds the same when you remove two letters?

104. What number do you get when you multiply all of the numbers on a telephone's number pad?

105. I have many voices but cannot speak. What am I?

106. What has cities but no houses, mountains but no trees, and water but no fish?

107. What occurs once in every minute, twice in every moment, yet never in a thousand years?

108. You walk into a room that has a bed. On the bed, there are five pigs, four chickens, and three dogs. How many legs are on the floor?

109. Mateo left home running. He ran a ways and then turned left, ran the same distance and turned left again, ran the same distance and turned left again. When he got home, there were two masked men. Who were they?

110. If two hours ago, it was as long after 1 PM as it was before 1 AM, what time is it now?

111. A sundial has the fewest moving parts of any timepiece. Which has the most?

112. When Lucia was eight, her little sister Sofia was half her age. Lucia is 30 now. How old is Sofia?

113. What is tall when it is young and short when it is old?

114. What is full of holes but still holds water?

115. What runs all around a backyard, yet never moves?

116. What has words, but never speaks?

117. What falls down but never gets hurt?

118. What has a bottom at the top?

119. What flies without wings?

120. What has 13 hearts but no organs?

121. What turns things around but never moves?

122. What do you throw out when you use it, but take back in when you are finished with it?

123. Why is it not legal for a man to marry his widow's sister?

124. Why can't a man living in Australia be buried in England?

125. A man shaves fifteen times a day but still has a beard. How?

126. A redhouse is made from red bricks. A bluehouse is made from blue bricks. A yellowhouse is made from yellow bricks. What is a greenhouse made from?

127. What is greater: half a quarter or quarter of a half?

128. A grandfather, two fathers and two sons went to get ice cream and everyone bought one ice cream cone each. How many ice cream cones did they buy in total?

129. What is the maximum number of times you can subtract 5 from 30?

130. If a papa bull eats three bales of hay and a baby bull eats one bale, how much hay will a mama bull eat?

131. What can be measured, but has no length, width, or height?

132. If it takes 3 people to dig 1 hole how many people does it takes to dig 1/2 a hole?

133. What instrument can you hear but never touch or see?

134. A brother and sister were sharing chicken nuggets. The sister had three times as many nuggets as her brother. After giving him one, she still had twice as many as him. How many more must she give him to even things out?

135. Two brothers start with the same number of toys. How many toys must the younger brother give the older brother for the older brother to have ten more toys than he does?

136. What is the difference between yesterday and tomorrow?

137. It's midnight and currently raining. The weather forecast predicts warm and sunny weather for the next two days. Will it be sunny in 48 hours?

trickier riddles questions

138. You have 100 white marbles, 100 black marbles, and two buckets. How can you best arrange the marbles to maximize the chance of drawing a single white marble from each bucket?

139. A man and his son were in an automobile accident. The man died but the boy was rushed to surgery. The surgeon said, "I can't operate on this child, he is my son." How is this possible?

140. I have seven candles lit. Two blew out. How many candles do I have left?

141. What goes around the house and in the house but never touches the house?

142. Two parents have six sons and each son has one sister. How many people are in the family?

143. A man once claimed he knew the score of every basketball game before it had even started, and he was always correct. How?

144. What thrives when you feed it but dies when you give it something to drink?

145. What's one question that nobody can honestly say "no" to?

146. Two men are caught in the rain and soaked from head to toe. Why did only one get his shoes wet?

147. What falls but never breaks, and what breaks but never falls?

148. Lose me once and I'll come back stronger. Lose me twice and I'll leave forever. What am I?

149. Five children in a class guessed how many shells were in a jar: Amy (36), Brenda (41), Clara (40), Dave (37), and Elliott (42). One person was right while one guess was off by 4, another by 3, another by 2, and another by 1. Who was correct?

150. I cannot talk, but I always reply when spoken to. What am I?

151. The person who makes it, sells it. The person who buys it never uses it. The person who uses it never knows they are using it. What is it?

152. What is so fragile that saying its name breaks it?

153. What comes once in a year, twice in a month, four times in a week, and six times in a day?

154. What is always coming but never arrives?

155. What can run but never walks, has a mouth but never talks, has a head but never weeps, has a bed but never sleeps?

156. What starts with an E, ends with an E, but only contains one letter?

157. What two things can you never eat for breakfast?

158. If you have one, you want to share it, but once you share it, you don't have it anymore. What is it?

159. What is something you will never see again?

160. Imagine you had a bag of candy. On the first day, you ate one-third of it. On the second day, you ate two pieces. On the third day, you had two pieces left. How many pieces did you start with?

161. If Mrs. Black's rooster lays an egg in Mr. Brown's yard, who owns the egg?

162. I'm lighter than air, but a hundred people can't lift me. What am I?

163. How many letters are then in the alphabet?

164. Twenty pigeons sat on the branches of a tree. A man shoots one pigeon with his gun. How many are now left on the tree?

165. An archaeologist found a coin dated 81 BC but knew it was fake. How?

166. What always ends everything?

167. What is the last year we have had which read the same upside down?

168. A bike wheel has 23 spokes. How many spaces are there between those spokes?

169. A 300-foot train is traveling 300 feet per minute must travel through a 300-foot-long tunnel. How long will it take the train to travel through the tunnel?

170. A duck was given $9, a spider was given $36, a bee was given $27. Based on this information, how much money would be given to a cat?

171. There is a basket containing 6 apples and there are 6 children. How can you give each child 1 apple while keeping 1 apple in the basket?

172. On a 12-hour digital clock, what is the smallest interval between two times that can both be read forwards and backwards as the same number?

173. What is made of wood, but can't be sawed?

174. Which two whole positive numbers make a single digit when multiplied but a double digit when added?

175. Imagine you are in a room with no windows or doors. How will you get out?

176. A taxi cab driver goes the wrong way down a one-way street. He passes the cops, but they don't stop him. Why?

177. If an electric train is traveling south, then which way is the smoke going?

178. At an intersection in New York City, four cars came to a four-way stop, each coming from a different direction. They couldn't decide who got there first, so they all went forward at the same time. All four cars went, but none crash into each other. How is that possible?

179. What do you bury when it's alive and dig up when it's dead?

180. I am a three-digit number. My tens digit is five more than my ones digit. My hundreds digit is eight less than my tens digit. What number am I?

181. When you try to put fish into separate fish bowls, you have one fish too many. When you try to put two fish into each fish bowl you have one fish bowl too many. How many fish and fish bowls do you have?

182. A father is three times as old as his son. In 10 years, he will be twice as old as his son. How old are the father and son now?

183. I'm always in sight when you stop and look, but you can never touch me. I am still, but as you approach you will not get closer. What am I?

184. What can you see in water but never gets wet?

185. There is an insect whose name begins with another insect's name. What is it?

186. How much dirt is there in a hole 2 meters deep, 3 meters wide and 4 meters long?

187. Which common English verb changes to its past tense by rearranging its letters?

188. How is it possible that with only two people, Jordan is the father of Alex, but Alex is not the son of Jordan?

trickier riddles questions

189. Take 110 marbles and make two sets where one set is 150% larger than the other. How many are in each set?

190. If you reverse the digits of a mother's age, you get her son's age. A year ago, the mother was twice as old as her son. What are their current ages?

191. In a town with only two barbers, one has perfectly groomed hair, while the other's hair is a complete mess. Which barber should you visit for the best haircut?

192. If a bike costs $20 more than a helmet, and their total cost is $50, how much does the helmet cost?

193. I am taken from a mine and shut up in a wooden case, from which I am never released, and yet I am used by almost every person. What am I?

194. You're escaping a maze, and there are three doors in front of you. The door on the left leads to a pit of lava. The door in the center leads to a room filled with deadly gas. The door on the right leads to a lion that hasn't eaten in three months. Which door do you choose?

195. You're in a dark room with a candle, a wood stove, and a gas lamp. You only have one match, so what do you light first?

196. You see a boat filled with people, yet there isn't a single person on board. How is that possible?

197. I have no life, but I can die. What am I?

198. A grandfather clock chimes 5 times in 4 seconds. How many times will it chime in 10 seconds?

199. You are in a house. There are five houses on the block. In each house, there are five cats. For each cat, there are five kittens. How many legs are there in total on the block?

200. Can you name three consecutive days without using Tuesday, Thursday, or Saturday?

trickier riddles questions

201. What is the most common use of cowhide?

202. A window cleaner is cleaning a window on the 25th floor of a skyscraper when, suddenly, he slips and falls. He has no safety equipment and yet he is uninjured. How can this be?

203. A man is alone in his house washing dishes. When he looks down, there are more glasses in the sink than there were before. How?

204. If you're buying amusement park tickets, is it cheaper to take one friend on two different days, or two friends on the same day?

205. If you were standing on the Nort h Pole and took a step backwards, which direction would you travel?

206. Is an older one-hundred-dollar bill worth more than a newer one?

207. What is 20 divided by 1/2 plus 10?

208. Put a coin into an empty bottle and insert a cork into the neck. How can you remove the coin without removing the cork or breaking the bottle?

209. What can fill a room but takes up no space?

210. Cooper and Asher each have their own sand piles. Cooper has six, and Asher has nine. When they combine their piles, how many do they have now?

211. The more you take, the more you leave behind. What are they?

212. What can you make that no one—not even you—can see?

213. A man wearing all black clothing is walking down a street with all the streetlights turned off. A black car approaches, with its headlights turned off, but manages to stop before hitting the man. How did the driver see him?

214. There are two planes. One is flying from New York to Los Angeles at a speed of 500 MPH. The other is traveling from Los Angeles to New York at a speed of 400 MPH. When the planes meet, which one will be closer to New York?

215. Which four letter word reads the same both forwards, backwards, the right way up and upside down?

216. You have a bin with 48 socks in white, black, or striped patterns. How many socks do you need to pull out to ensure you get a matching pair?

217. You are reading a book that is four hundred pages long. If you read half of the remaining book each day, how many days will it take you to finish?

218. A person is sitting in their house at night reading but there are no sources of light. How?

219. Find the tree mistake in this sentence.

220. A cowboy rode into town on Friday, stayed three days, and then left on Friday. How?

221. Why are these numbers in this order? 8, 5, 4, 9, 1, 7, 6, 10, 3, 2, 0.

222. How can you make eight 8s add up to 1,000?

223. Two men play seven complete games of chess. Each man wins the same number of games and there are no ties. How?

224. A child was ten on their last birthday, and will be twelve on their next birthday. How is this possible?

225. When John was six years old he hammered a nail into his favorite tree to mark his height. Ten years later at age sixteen, John returned to see how much higher the nail was. If the tree grew by five centimeters each year, how much higher would the nail be?

226. Three times what number is no larger than two times the same number?

227. A hotel has eight floors. Four people live on the ground floor, and each floor has two more people living on it than the previous level. Which floor calls the elevator the most?

228. What can you put between a 4 and a 5 to make the result greater than a 4 but less than a 5?

229. There are five people in an empty, circular room. Each person has full sight of the entire room and everyone in it without turning his head or body or moving in any way. Where can you place a banana so that all but one person can see it?

230. Where can everyone sit on except you?

231. You're on a bus. 10 people get on at the first stop. At the next stop 35 people get on. At the third stop 38 people get off. Then at the next stop 3 people get off and 5 get on. At the last stop 9 people get off and then only you and one other person is left. How is this possible?

232. How can two people born simultaneously have different birthdays?

233. How do you use four 9s, a 1, and a math operator to equal 100?

234. How is it possible that a man sitting in his cabin in Florida can get out of his cabin in Texas three hours later?

235. What is in everything and also in nothing?

236. James drove East to visit his friend at 60 miles per hour. On the return trip West, he drove at 30 miles per hour to enjoy the scenery. What was his average speed for the entire trip?

237. Sophia took a 20-question test with 2 points for each correct answer and a 1 point deduction for each incorrect answer. She answered all questions and scored 25 points. How many questions did she miss?

238. In a field with only cows and chickens, there are 38 heads and 128 legs. How many cows and chickens are there?

239. You're bringing chocolates to a friend's house and cross 5 checkpoints. At each one, you must give up half of your chocolates, but each guard gives you back one chocolate. How many chocolates must you begin with to give your friend 2 chocolates?

240. Mason and Lily are neighbors. After a heavy snowfall, Lily's yard has twice as much snow as Mason's. Why?

241. It takes 6 minutes to grill a hamburger— 3 minutes on each side. Your grill can hold only two burgers at a time. What's the shortest time to grill 3 burgers?

242. A man describes his daughters saying, "They all have red hair but two, they all have brown hair but two, and they all have black hair but two." How many daughters does he have?

243. Roman numeral IX is equal to 9. How can you transform IX into six by adding one line?

244. Amina works in a store. One day, a mute woman walks up to her and mimics brushing her teeth. Amina immediately understands she wants a toothbrush. Next, a deaf man approaches Amina. How can he explain that he wants a comb?

245. James and Aaron race each other in a 100-yard dash. James wins by 10 yards. They decide to race again, but to make things fair James starts 10 yards behind Aaron. If they both run exactly the same speed as before, who wins the race?

246. Two sailors were standing on opposite sides of the ship. One was looking West and the other one East, yet they could see each other clearly. How?

247. In 1990, a person is 15 years old. In 1995, that same person is 10 years old. How can this be?

248. If six cats catch six mice in six minutes, how long will it take 30 cats to catch 30 mice?

249. In a forest, there is a patch of mushrooms. Every day, the patch doubles in size. If it takes 28 days for the patch to cover the entire forest floor, how long would it take for the patch to cover half of the forest floor?

250. What can go up a chimney down, but not down a chimney up?

251. If there are two people in front of two others, two behind two others, and two beside two others, what is the smallest number of people there could be?

252. There are two cars in front of a car, two cars behind a car, and a car in the middle. How many cars are there?

253. What is heavy when forwards but backwards is not?

254. Which word changes both gender and number when the letter 's' is added?

255. How do you make the number 7 even without addition, subtraction, multiplication, or division?

256. If a hen and a half lay an egg and a half in a day and a half, how many eggs will half a dozen hens lay in half a dozen days?

257. A ladder hangs over the side of a ship anchored in port. The bottom rung of the ladder touches the water. The distance between rungs is 30cm, and the length of the ladder is 270cm. If the tide is rising at a rate of 15cm per hour, how long will it be before the water reaches the top rung?

258. What 5-letter word typed in all capital letters can be read the same upside down?

259. How many sides does a circle have?

260. A boy was at a carnival and went to a booth where a man said to the boy, "If I write your exact weight on this piece of paper then you have to give me $10, but if I cannot, I will pay you $10." The boy saw no scale so he agreed, thinking no matter what the carny writes he'll just say he weighs more or less. In the end the boy ended up paying the man $10. How did the man win the bet?

261. How do you spell candy in just two letters?

262. A girl is turning twelve this year but turned eleven yesterday. How could that be possible?

263. Two trains entered a single-track tunnel from opposite ends at 8 o'clock. Three minutes later, they both emerged safely. How did they avoid a collision?

264. A robber demands the code to a bank safe. The teller says, "I can't give it to you. The code is changing every day." Yet, the robber figures it out. How did he do it?

265. 123456789123456789123456789. Can you find the the mistake?

266. What can you take away the whole from, yet still have some left?

267. When is "L" larger in size that "XL"?

268. What is it that given one, you'll have either some or none?

269. In a 10-page paper, the first page says, "Exactly one page in this paper is false." The second page says, "Exactly two pages in this paper are false." This pattern continues up to the tenth page. Do any of the pages contain a true statement?

270. What number is 5 less than a tenth of a fifth of a fourth of 1,000?

271. You brought some cupcakes to a party. Your friends ate half of them plus half a cupcake, leaving you with one cupcake. How many did you originally bring?

272. How can you make 8 + 8 = 91 correct without removing or adding anything?

273. Emma and Liam played table tennis, betting $1 per game. Emma won four games, and Liam ended up $6 ahead. How many games did they play?

274. Two men needed to cross a river, but their boat could only hold one person and it couldn't return on its own. How did both men manage to cross using the boat?

275. There are two children, one boy and one girl. One has brown hair and the other is blonde. The child with brown hair says, "I am a boy." The child with blonde hair says, "I am a girl." At least one of them is lying. Who is the boy and who is the girl?

276. Five teams played a round-robin basketball tournament where each team played each other team once. Wins earned 2 points while ties awarded 1 point to each team. If the finishing points totals were: Alligators (5), Bears (3), Cougars (5), Ducks (4), how many points did the Eagles end with?

277. You have nine balls, and one is heavier than the others. How can you find the heavy ball using only two times to weigh on a balance scale?

278. Three people are trapped on a plateau surrounded on all sides by a 100-foot-deep ravine that is 100 feet wide. All they have is a 30-foot-tall ladder, a 10-foot-tall ladder, a can of gasoline, a lighter, and however much rope they need. How do they get across?

279. If you throw me out a window, you'll leave a grieving wife. But stick me in a door, and I can save a life. What am I?

280. What English word has six letters, but if you take away one, you're left with twelve?

281. You find yourself at an unmarked intersection, with one path leading to the City of Lies and the other to the City of Truth. Citizens of the City of Lies always lie, while those from the City of Truth always tell the truth. You encounter a citizen from one of these cities, but you don't know which. What question can you ask to determine the way to the City of Truth?

282. How can four be half of five?

283. Six glasses are in a row. The first three a full and the next three are empty. How can you move only one glass so they alternate between full and empty?

284. A man steals a $50 bill from a cash register without the shop owner noticing and then buys $30 worth of good using the stolen $50. The owner gives him $20 in change. How much money did the owner lose?

trickiest riddles questions

285. Two brothers are told by their father's will that the slower horse in their race will win the inheritance. Both brothers hold back, causing a stalemate. When they consult a wise man, his advice leads them to race quickly. What did he say?

286. Three people check into a hotel room that costs $30. They each contribute $10, handing $30 to the hotel clerk. Later, the hotel clerk realizes that there was a mistake, and the room only costs $25. The hotel clerk gives $5 to the bellboy and asks him to return it to the guests. However, the bellboy decides to keep $2 for himself and gives $1 back to each guest. Now, each guest has paid $9 (totaling $27) and the bellboy has kept $2, making $29. What happened to the missing dollar?

287. You have three boxes, one containing only apples, one only oranges, and one a mix of both. Each box is labeled incorrectly. You can pick one fruit from one box. How can you correctly label all the boxes?

288. How do you make the number one disappear by adding to it?

289. How can you accurately measure two minutes using only a three-minute, four-minute, and five-minute sand timer?

290. How can you evenly divide two apples among three people with just one cut?

291. How can you measure exactly four gallons using only water, a three-gallon jar, and a five-gallon jar?

292. In a group of 100 people, each person is either honest or a liar. You know that at least one person is honest and that amongst any pair of people, at least one is a liar. How many liars are there?

293. How can you position four objects so that each one is the same distance from the others?

294. I have four or more children. I have fewer than four children. I have at least one child. If only one of these statements is true, how many children do I have?

295. You have a large cube composed of 10x10x10 smaller cubes, making a total of 1,000 cubes. If you remove the outer layer, how many cubes are left?

296. Which is greater: six dozen dozens or half a dozen dozens?

trickiest riddles questions

297. You have a total of 4 pills consisting of two pills of two different types. All the pills look the same. How can you ensure that you take 1 pill of each type both days?

298. How can you plant 10 trees to form five rows, each with four trees?

299. How many letters are in the answer to this riddle?

300. Four friends need to cross a bridge, but only two can cross at a time. It's a dark night and they only have one flashlight which is needed to make any crossings. Chloe takes 1 minute to cross, Jack takes 2 minutes, Layla takes 4 minutes, and Benjamin takes 8 minutes. What's the fastest they can all get across?

TRICKY RIDDLES ANSWERS

1. Water.

2. Y.

3. A clock.

4. An onion.

5. A kite.

6. A donut.

7. A freezer.

8. A belly button.

9. A bar of soap.

10. A bottle.

11. Darkness or fog.

12. The library.

13. Nothing.

14. Your luck.

15. There are no stairs, it's a one-story house.

16. A compass.

17. Corn.

18. A bank.

19. No one is lying because the three doctors are Paul's sisters.

20. A cold.

21. A coin.

22. A rubber band.

23. 20: 7, 17, 27, 37, 47, 57, 67, 70, 71, 72, 73, 74, 75, 76, 77, 78, 79, 87, 97.

24. A cloud.

25. Popcorn.

26. He's playing Monopoly.

27. A needle.

28. Incorrectly.

29. A staircase.

30. A joke.

31. A pair of scissors.

32. None.

33. A mushroom.

34. Wrong.

35. A towel.

36. Your age.

37. A garbage truck.

38. A window.

39. Trouble.

40. Someone's heart or emotions.

41. A tissue.

42. A dictionary.

43. A tongue.

44. A shadow.

45. Wind.

46. Gloves or mittens.

47. A wheel.

48. A boxing ring.

49. A skull.

50. Bread.

51. A piano or keyboard.

52. A comb.

53. All of them.

54. You now have two apples and I have one.

55. Stars.

56. A promise.

57. A hole.

58. 1, 2, and 3.

59. A table.

60. It was still Mount Everest, it just hadn't been discovered yet.

61. A shirt or sweater.

62. Halfway. After that, he's running back out of the woods.

63. Your breath.

64. The future.

65. Plants.

66. The spare tire.

67. Your brain.

68. Your name.

69. Your word.

70. A coat of paint.

71. Your right hand/elbow.

72. A telephone.

73. Plates and cutlery.

74. A match.

75. Fingerprints.

76. Water.

77. A pillow.

78. Zero.

79. A flag.

80. A doorbell or a telephone.

81. When the water is frozen.

82. Fifth.

83. Six.

84. 99.

85. He fell from the bottom rung.

86. Every year.

87. Dry stones.

88. A stamp.

89. The man was bald.

90. The letter "R".

91. A teapot.

92. A road.

93. The other end of the rope isn't tied to anything.

94. What time is it?

95. You draw a shorter line next to it, and then it becomes the longer line.

96. Four.

97. A tennis ball, volleyball, or pickleball.

98. Knowledge.

99. 18 seconds, since you need to make 9 cuts.

100. Syllables.

101. *Leaves.*

102. *An ice cube.*

103. *Pea.*

104. *Zero. Anything multiplied by 0 will equal 0.*

105. *A radio or television.*

106. *A map.*

107. *The letter "M".*

108. *There are six legs on the floor—your own two legs and the bed's four legs.*

109. *The catcher and the umpire.*

110. *9PM.*

111. *An hourglass. It has thousands of grains of sand.*

112. *Sofia is 26.*

113. *A candle.*

114. *A sponge.*

115. *A fence.*

116. *A book.*

117. *Rain or snow.*

118. Your legs.

119. Time.

120. A deck of cards.

121. A mirror.

122. An anchor.

123. You cannot marry someone if you are dead.

124. Because he is still living.

125. He is a barber.

126. Glass.

127. They are the same.

128. 3 (the grandfather is also a father and the father is also a son).

129. Once. After you subtract 5 from 30, it then becomes 25. So, from that point on, you can no longer subtract from 30.

130. A bull is a male cow so there is no such thing as a mama bull.

131. Temperature.

132. You can't dig 1/2 an hole because once you begin to dig it is an hole.

133. Voice.

134. Two. She started with nine nuggets, and he started with three.

135. 5.

136. Today.

137. No, because it will be midnight in 48 hours.

138. Place one white marble in one bucket, and all the remaining marbles in the other bucket. This way, you'll always draw a white marble from the first bucket and have nearly a 50% chance of drawing a white marble from the second bucket.

139. The surgeon was the boy's mother.

140. Seven — just because you blow the candle out doesn't mean they disappear.

141. The sun.

142. Nine: two parents, six sons, and one daughter.

143. He always said 0-0, because that the score at the start of the game.

144. A fire.

145. Are you awake?

146. Because only one was wearing shoes; the other was barefoot.

147. Night and day (nightfall and daybreak).

148. A tooth.

149. Clara with 40.

150. An echo.

151. A coffin.

152. Silence.

153. The letter "E".

154. Tomorrow.

155. A river.

156. An envelope.

157. Lunch and dinner.

158. A secret.

159. Yesterday.

160. 6.

161. Roosters don't lay eggs.

162. A bubble.

163. "The alphabet" has 11 letters.

164. *None – they would all fly away because of the noise.*

165. *People living in BC times didn't know that they were BC times.*

166. *The letter "G".*

167. *1961.*

168. *23.*

169. *Two minutes. It takes the front of the train one minute and the rest of the train will take two minutes to clear the tunnel.*

170. *$18 ($4.50 per leg).*

171. *Give the last child the basket with one apple in it.*

172. *Two minutes – between the times of 9:59 and 10:01.*

173. *Sawdust.*

174. *1 and 9.*

175. *Stop imagining.*

176. *He was walking.*

177. *There is no smoke from an electric train.*

178. *They all made right-hand turns.*

179. A plant.

180. 194.

181. Four fish and three fish bowls.

182. The father is 30, the son is 10.

183. The horizon.

184. A reflection or shadow.

185. Beetle.

186. None. It is a hole.

187. Eat and ate.

188. Alex is girl.

189. 44 and 66.

190. 73 and 37.

191. The one with messy hair, as they are the one who cuts the neat barber's hair.

192. $15.

193. Pencil lead.

194. The door on the right. A lion that hasn't eaten in three months would be dead.

195. The match.

196. *All the people on the boat are married.*

197. *A battery.*

198. *The clock will chime 12 times in 10 seconds.*

199. *602 (100 legs from cats, 500 legs from kittens, 2 legs from you).*

200. *Yesterday, today, and tomorrow.*

201. *Covering cows.*

202. *He is cleaning the window from the inside.*

203. *His own pair of eyeglasses fell into the sink.*

204. *It's cheaper to take two friends on the same day because you only need to buy three tickets, instead of four.*

205. *South.*

206. *A $100 bill is worth more than a $1 bill (newer one).*

207. *50 ("divide 20 by 1/2" means 20 ÷ (1/2) which is equal to 40, then add 10).*

208. *Push the cork down into the bottle. Then shake the coin out.*

209. *Light.*

210. *One single pile.*

211. *Footsteps.*

212. *Noise.*

213. *It was daytime.*

214. *They will be in the same spot when they meet and therefore both the same distance from New York.*

215. NOON.

216. Four. Pulling out a fourth sock will ensure that at least one of the socks will match one of the three you already have if the first three were all different.

217. You would never finish. There would always be something left if you only ever read half.

218. The person is blind and reading braille.

219. Tree should be 'three'. Mistake should be 'mistakes'. There are only two mistakes.

220. The horse was named Friday.

221. They are in alphabetical order.

222. 888 + 88 + 8 + 8 +8.

223. The two men were not playing against each other.

224. Today is their eleventh birthday.

225. The nail would be at the same height since trees grow at their tops.

226. Zero.

227. *The ground floor. Everyone living on the other floors will still need to call the elevator to the ground floor to then get on and get to their own floors.*

228. *The answer is a decimal. 4.5 is greater than 4 but less than 5.*

229. *On one person's head.*

230. *On your lap.*

231. *You and the bus driver are still on the bus.*

232. *They are born in different time zones resulting in different days.*

233. *199 – 99.*

234. *He is a pilot in the cabin of an airplane.*

235. *The letter "T".*

236. *40 miles per hour. Since his return trip took twice as long at half the speed, the average is calculated as (60 + 30 + 30) ÷ 3 = 40.*

237. *5.*

238. *26 cows and 12 chickens.*

239. *2. Each time you give the guard 1 and they return 1 back to you.*

240. Lily's yard is twice the size.

241. 9 minutes. Grill two burgers for 3 minutes on one side. Flip one, remove the other, and start the third. After another 3 minutes, the first is done. Finally, flip the third and put the second back on the grill for 3 minutes.

242. Three.

243. Add an "S" before IX and you have SIX.

244. He asks for it. He is deaf, not mute.

245. James will win again. In the first race James ran 100 yards in the time it took Aaron to run 90. Therefore, in the second race, once Aaron has run 90 yards they will both be side by side. Since James runs faster, he will take less time to run the last 10 yards than Aaron and will therefore win.

246. The sailors had their backs against either ends of the ship.

247. The person was born in 2005 BC.

248. Six minutes.

249. 27 days.

250. An umbrella.

251. Four. (In a square).

252. Three. Two cars are in front of the last car; the first car has two cars behind; one car is between the other two.

253. Ton.

254. Princes (changes to princess).

255. Drop the "S" from seven.

256. Two dozen. The ratio of hens to eggs stays the same. If 1.5 hens lay 1.5 eggs in 1.5 days, then 6 hens (which is four times more hens) in 6 days (which is also four times more days) will lay 16 times more eggs. Therefore, they will lay 24 eggs in total.

257. The ship will rise with the tide, so the water will always remain level with the first rung.

258. SWIMS.

259. Two. Inside and outside.

260. The man wrote "your exact weight" on the paper.

261. C and y: c(and)y.

262. If the current day is January 1st of the next year and her birthday is on December 31.

263. One train comes at 8am and the other train came at 8pm.

264. The code is "changing".

265. In the question, "the" is written twice.

266. Wholesome.

267. In Roman numerals.

268. A choice.

269. Yes. The statement on page 9 would be true.

270. Zero (1,000 ÷ 10 = 100 ÷ 5 = 20 ÷ 4 = 5 – 5 = 0).

271. 3.

272. Turn it upside down: 16 = 8 + 8.

273. 14 games. If Emma won the first four, Liam was down $4. It took 10 more games for him to win $6 overall.

274. They started on opposite sides of the river.

275. They both lied. The child with brown hair is the girl, and the blonde-haired child is the boy. If only one of them had lied, both would have had to be either boys or girls.

276. *3. There were 10 matches and each match awarded 2 points for a total of 20.*

277. *First, weigh three balls against three other balls. If they balance, the heavy ball is among the three not weighed. If they don't balance, the heavy ball is in the heavier group of three. Next, weigh two balls from the heavy group. If they balance, the heavy ball is the third one. If they don't, the heavier ball is found.*

278. *They fill the ravine with as much as rope as they need until it reaches the top, then walk across.*

279. *The letter "N" (window → widow, door → donor).*

280. *Dozens.*

281. *Ask, "In which direction do you live?" Both a liar and a truth-teller will point to the City of Truth.*

282. *If it is written in Roman numerals as IV, which two of the four letters used to spell FIVE.*

283. *Pour the second glass into the fifth glass.*

284. $50. The owner is down $50 when the money is stolen and is down $30 worth of goods. Then gets back $50 when the customer pays and then loses $20 when giving change (-$50 -$30 +$50 - $20 = -$50).

285. To switch horses. Whoever wins the race will get the inheritance because they still own the losing (slower) horse.

286. There is no missing dollar. The guests have paid a total of $27 ($25 to the hotel and $2 to the bellboy).

287. Pick a fruit from the "mixed" box. Whatever fruit you pick, that's the actual content of that box. Use logic to correctly label the other two.

288. Add a "G" and it is gone.

289. Flip the three-minute and five-minute timers at the same time. When the three-minute timer runs out, two minutes remain on the five-minute timer. The four-minute timer isn't needed.

290. Stack the two apples and cut 1/3 off each apple so that each person gets 2/3 of an apple.

291. Fill the five-gallon jar entirely, then pour its contents into the three-gallon jar until it is full. Empty the three-gallon jar. Pour the remaining two gallons from the five-gallon jar into the three-gallon jar. Refill the five-gallon jar and pour into the three-gallon jar until it is full. This leaves you with four gallons in the five-gallon jar.

292. 99. If each pair must include at least one liar, then when you pair the one honest person with each of the other 99 people, each of those must be a liar.

293. Place three of them in an equilateral triangle and the fourth one in the middle of that triangle on an elevated surface (to form a tetrahedron).

294. None. If any of the statements about having children were true, it would make two statements true. Therefore, I have no children.

295. 512 cubes. The remaining cube will measure 8x8x8.

296. Six dozen dozens is greater. 6 x 12 x 12 = 864, while (0.5 x 12) x 12 = 72.

297. Cut each pill in half and take half of each both days.

298. Arrange them in the shape of a five-pointed star.

299. Four – it's the only number whose name has the same number of letters as the number itself, making it the only true answer.

300. 15 minutes. Chloe and Jack cross the bridge first, taking 2 minutes. Chloe then returns with the flashlight, making it 3 minutes. Next, Layla and Benjamin cross together, using up 8 minutes, which totals to 11 minutes. Jack then goes back with the flashlight, adding 2 more minutes and making it 13 minutes. Finally, Chloe and Jack cross together, which takes the last 2 minutes, bringing the total time to 15 minutes.

BEFORE YOU GO

Thank you for choosing *Brainteasers and Riddles for Gritty Kids*. I hope you and your family have enjoyed the mental workouts and fun challenges within these pages.

If you found joy and value in this book, **I would be immensely grateful if you could take a moment to leave a review on Amazon**. Your feedback not only helps other parents and educators discover this book, but it also plays a vital role in supporting *Gritty Kids®*.

For any comments or suggestions, I would love to hear from you. Please feel free to reach out at info@greenmeeplebooks.com.

Your input is greatly valued. The *Gritty Kids®* series have been edited and revised thanks to helpful suggestions from readers.

Gritty and grateful,
Dan Allbaugh

Made in the USA
Las Vegas, NV
10 January 2025

16222158R00037